Antique Mall Profits

for Dealers and Dabblers

Wayne Jordan

Copyright

Table of Contents

Introduction: The Profit Trap

There's a myth that is pervasive among antique and vintage dealers that gets them into trouble faster than any other single issue. Here it is:

Profits = Cash.

Sounds right, doesn't it? Most myths do. It stands to reason that if you buy low and sell high, you'll make a profit, and the profit will go right into your bank account as spendable cash, right? Right; until you spend some of it on inventory. When you buy inventory, you're investing profits back into your business. Some re-investment is necessary and good, but if taken too far it can fast-track you right into bankruptcy court.

Here's an all-too-common scenario:

Imagine that you're in business with your cousin Ralph.

You open a booth in a nice location with a starting inventory of $5,000 at cost. You pay your bills on time and both you and Ralph take very little money out of the business, preferring instead to boost the amount of inventory you have on hand so you can sell more and make more money. At the end of your first year, you've stayed on top of the bills and raised your inventory level to $15,000.

You get the year-end books from your accountant and they show a net profit of $10,000 for the first year. "That's fantastic!" says Ralph. "Cut me a check for my half so I can make a down-payment on a bass boat".

"I can't cut you a check" you say; "we don't have that kind of money in the checking account".

"How can that be?" asks Ralph. We have a $10,000 profit! Where did all the money go?"

Well, the answer is obvious, isn't it? The money is sitting in your booth, disguised as inventory.

But for you and Cousin Ralph, the story just gets interesting.

As long as you're selling enough, you'll have enough cash to pay your bills. But first you must pay taxes on the $10,000 profit. Depending on how your business is set up and what your other income is, taxes will be about $2,000-$3,000. You don't have the cash, so the squeeze is on.

If sales drop off, you'll really be in trouble; and that's just what happens: sales drop off. Only a portion of your inventory is selling quickly, and the rest just sits there. So, Ralph attempts to buy more of what is selling, sometimes using personal funds to do so.

In fairness to Ralph, it's hard to predict with any accuracy what consumers will buy; you can get an idea with a little research, but you never know for sure. Some of your new inventory sells, some of it doesn't. Meanwhile, your unsold inventory gets older with every month and the amount of unsold inventory grows. And every month you're getting farther and farther behind on your bills.

Are you profitable? Yes. Do you have enough cash to pay your bills? No, because all your cash is tied up in inventory. You've fallen into the Profit Trap and getting out of it won't be easy. Like all traps, it's best to avoid them. The profit trap can be avoided with a little advance planning.

New retailers soon learn that profits aren't always represented as cash on a balance sheet. The number one job for any retailer—big or small—is to control their inventory. Lose control of your inventory and you lose control of your business. Control your inventory and you will find that you have enough cash to enjoy the benefits of business ownership.

This book is designed with one purpose in mind: to help antique dealers make the connection between their inventory and their money. Inventory—buying it, pricing it, displaying it, and selling it—is at the core of a dealers "business puzzle". Dealers who do not grasp inventory essentials will struggle and risk failure, and it won't be because they can't make a profit. Forty percent of small businesses that declare bankruptcy are profitable; they just run out of cash.

In Antique Mall Profits, I'll point out a few of the common traps that new retailers—and some old-timers—fall into. Once you know what the traps look like, you'll be able to avoid them. If you already find yourself in a financial tight spot, you'll learn a few tactics that will put you back on solid ground. Here's a sample of what you'll learn in this book:

- How to know if you should buy an item or walk away from it.

- How to make your booth stand out from the competition.

- Eight tactics that will turn your booth into a selling powerhouse.

- Five tips for buying right: practice these techniques and you'll seldom overpay for inventory.

- A simple formula for knowing how much inventory you'll need. Never be stuck with dead inventory again!

- How much you must charge to make a profit.

- Ten pricing tactics that will keep your inventory moving.

- Five strategies to sell more without taking markdowns.

- When—and how much—to take markdowns; timing is everything!

This book presupposes that you already know something about antiques. I won't tell you which items you should stock or what items are hot sellers; all that information is available elsewhere. My purpose here is to present the basics of running a profitable mall booth. Although my focus is Antique Mall dealers, the principles apply to retail stores of any type or size.

Chapter One: More Profit, Less Competition

If you're an antique dealer (or are dreaming about becoming one), then congratulations: You've picked the right business. The antiques and vintage business is hands-down the best small retail business to be in at the moment.

Consider the problems faced by other, non-antique Main Street retailers: In the past twenty years, Big Box stores have put scores of Mom and Pop commodity retailers out of business. Why? Because the Mom and Pops are selling the same products as the Big Box stores, but they don't have the advantage of Big Box buying power. Mom and Pops can't compete with Big Box prices.

Not so with antiques, collectibles or art dealers. The inventory of such dealers offers variety and uniqueness. Unlike commodity dealers, antique dealers can't just pick up the phone and order a gross more of the latest hot seller. Antique dealers put their "picking" skills to work daily to find their stock one item at a time. In the antiques trade, there are no discounts for buying in bulk. Antique and vintage dealers pay what they want to pay for merchandise and sell it for the price they want to get. No one tells them what they must pay, or what they must charge. There will never be competition from Big Box retailers of antiques, because there will be no Big Box retailers of antiques.

And, business is good. In February 2019, the research company IBISWorld reported[1] that used merchandise sales in the U.S. totaled $19 billion. Antiques and collectibles generate $5 billion per year in online sales alone. The antiques and collectibles trade generates big-business revenues from small independent dealers.

Consider a few other pluses of being in the antiques and vintage trade:

- **The barriers to entry are low**: if your funds are limited you can start by selling a few items online and grow your business from there.

- **The economy is turning in favor of antique and vintage goods**. In a November 2017 whitepaper, Cascade Alliance[2] reported: "Whether the economy is

---

[1] ibisworld.com/industry-trends/market-research-reports/retail-trade/miscellaneous-store-retailers/used-goods-stores.html
[2] cascadealliance.us/wp-content/uploads/Thrift-store-white-paper-V.3-November-2017-.pdf

shrinking or expanding, used merchandise sales outperform that of the broader retail sector. Sales at resale stores increased over fifty percent between 2008-2016, at the same time discount department store revenues fell by half and traditional department stores lost one quarter of their sales, according to the U.S. Census Bureau statistics."

- **Antique and vintage dealers get better profit margins** for their wares than almost any other type of retail store. According to published benchmarks[3], used merchandise retailers have out-performed most other retailers in three major categories every year for the past five years.

The antiques business isn't all fun and games. Retail is a challenging trade, whether you sell online, at an antique mall, flea market, or bricks-and-mortar store. The good news is that if you manage your inventory and your cash, most issues that arise are manageable. That means buying right, selling at a profitable price, and getting a good return for your inventory investment.

The biggest competition that an antique dealer has is himself; not the other antique dealers in the building, not online sellers, not the big flea market across town. Antique dealers fail because, although they

---

[3] retailownersinstitute.com/Benchmarks/Other-Specialty-Retail-Stores/Used-Merchandise-Stores/lc/76081/retailers-get-financial-know-how-from-the-roi

know their merchandise well, they don't understand how the pieces of the "business puzzle" fit together.

Chapter Two: Why Sell at an Antique Mall?

Antique shops as we know them have been around since the late 19th Century (about the time the European Aristocracy started selling off their family heirlooms). Although single-owner, bricks-and-mortar antique shops still abound, they aren't as popular as they were 30 years ago. Consumer shopping preferences have transformed in the past 30 years: modern consumers demand selection and convenience. Consumers are no longer willing to drive from one Mom-and-Pop store to another to find items they are interested in buying.

In the early twentieth century department stores represented the height of retail development. In the 1950s, strip centers (a collection of stores along a highway) became popular. In the 1960s, open air shopping plazas were the rage. In the 1970s, indoor shopping malls became popular. In the 1980s, Big Box stores like Wal-Mart arrived on the scene.

The 1980s also saw the beginning of antique malls. Antique malls offer consumers a broad range of goods and prices all under one roof. Like Big Box stores, antique malls have what I like to call "gravity": They attract shoppers in the same way terrestrial bodies fall to Earth. Antique enthusiasts can drive from one Mom-and-Pop shop to another, or they can drive to an antique mall and browse a large selection offered by dozens (sometimes hundreds) of individual dealers. Some consumers shop both types of store, but if time is limited they will shop at the antique mall and skip the smaller shops.

Why sell at an antique mall? In one word: traffic. Consumer traffic is what retailers crave, and it can be had at an antique mall.

For new retailers, an antique mall offers substantial benefits over a traditional bricks-and-mortar store, such as:

- Lower initial investment

- It can be operated with a part-time commitment

- No employees needed

- No credit card processing hassles

- No long-term commercial lease

- Built-in traffic and reputation

- No point-of-sale software or cash register

- Lower merchandising costs

Another compelling benefit of operating an antique mall booth is that mall booths lend themselves to growth. When you have raised one booth to profitability, you can expand into another. By opening another mall booth in a different part of town (or another town altogether) you can tap into an entirely new market.

There's money to be made in an antique mall booth. But, to make a profit you must treat your booth like a business, not a hobby. If you treat your booth like it's a hobby—working it only when and if you feel like it—then it will give you the same financial return that a hobby does; which is to say, none.

The difference between being successful with your antique mall booth and shutting it down in your first year is a matter of understanding the basics of retailing. You can have the prettiest, most unique booth in the entire mall but if you do not apply a few basic financial principles then you will have nothing more than a pretty failure.

The most important consideration in starting a retail business is its location. These days, you'll find successful antique and vintage dealers operating from freestanding stores, strip shopping centers, flea markets, antique shows, and almost every venue where people gather. What's so special about setting up shop in an antique mall booth? Let's investigate that point in the next chapter.

Chapter Three: Location, Location, Location

Most of us are familiar with the real estate maxim "the three most important considerations in real estate are location, location, and location".

Since an antique mall is inseparable from its real estate, we had better pay attention to the above maxim when choosing a mall in which to locate. Once we have found a suitable mall, we should be equally concerned about finding a suitable location within the mall.

Selecting the mall location

The best locations for antique malls are those that are near a highway or well-travelled route, in a historic district, or near a tourist attraction. These locations are best because they attract a steady stream of new customers and out-of-town money. Malls outside of these locations attract local customers and lack the "new money" element that dealers seek. Highway travelers who need to stretch their legs may pull off the highway and spend an hour or so browsing the aisles of an antique mall. When an antique mall is in a tourist or historic area, antiquing becomes part of a visitor's recreational agenda. To visitors, an antique dealer's inventory appears new and fresh, and curiosity prompts them to investigate

How big should a mall be?

There's a long-running discussion among dealers about whether a big mall (over 100 dealers) produces more sales than a smaller, boutique-sized mall (under 50 dealers). Size takes a back seat to the questions "how much traffic does the mall get" and "does the booth rent reflect the level of traffic?" When a dealer pays rent, he's (she's) not paying for space, but for traffic. A dealer who has a prime booth space in a mall with no traffic won't sell much. When choosing a mall location, consider its traffic count foremost.

Leases are not for sissies

A lease is a legal document. If you sign a one-year lease that requires you to pay the landlord $300/month, then you owe the landlord $3,600 the minute you sign it. If you close your booth two months into the lease, you still owe for ten more months. The only way to get out of a lease is to declare bankruptcy, and I wouldn't recommend that. With leases, shorter is better. Usually, when the initial lease term ends you are put on a month-to-month payment schedule.

What about competing dealers?

Having dealers who sell in the same categories as you is a good thing. Why? Because consumers love a good value; they love to compare prices and quality. They want to choose from a selection of offerings. That's why the activity is called "shopping", not "buying". When collectors and antique enthusiasts discover that there is a good selection of their favorite items at your mall, and that dealers compete for their business, they will return often. Ultimately, you will sell more when competition is strong. You don't want to be the only antique tool dealer in a mall full of art & decor dealers.

Look for a frank and open mall management

There are several things that you must know before you sign a mall lease: traffic count, annual mall revenue, average sales per booth, and the range of sales (low to high) per booth. If management can't (or won't) give you that information, you will take a big risk by signing their lease. Remember, although the mall thinks you are paying for their space, what you are paying for is their traffic: You want eyes on your merchandise, not a just place to store your inventory.

Professionally managed antique malls know how many customers come through their doors in the course of a month, and they should give you that information. They also know what their mall's annual sales are, because they must remit sales tax to the state. If management claims not to know their average sales per booth, ask them for the annual sales for the mall as a whole and divide that amount by the number of dealers in the mall to get the average per booth.

If mall management claims to not have any of the above information, then they're not paying attention. If you wanted to rent space in a new, fancy retail mall (not an antique mall) the mall management would give you that information and even break it down to the traffic count past any storefront.

You must decide for yourself whether management is being evasive or is just unaware of the facts. Exercise your best judgment about whether you want to lease space there.

How friendly are the other dealers?

Like buying a house in a residential neighborhood, your neighbors directly affect your experience. Although you don't have to like the other dealers in the mall to do business there, it helps. In this regard, (if you sign a lease) be proactive. If a neighbor needs help moving a piece of furniture, give him a hand.

Security

Theft happens. Break-ins occur. Be sure that any mall you rent in has a good security system. If you sell small goods that are easy to steal, buy or rent a lockable display case.

Technology

Does your mall offer WiFi? Is there good cell phone reception? Today's retail shoppers love to "showroom"; that is, check prices and product features online before they buy. Consumer showrooming helps you sell more. Make sure that your customers can get online, whether through WiFi or via their smartphones.

Where to locate your booth within a mall

Just as the value of real estate in your city is determined by its location, the value of a booth in an antique mall can be measured by its location. Some booths will sell more than others because they are more noticeable.

Professionally managed malls understand that there is a correlation between the location and size of a booth and the revenue that it can create. So, they charge more rent for well-placed booth space, besides charging for the size of a booth.

Unfortunately, most antique malls are not professionally managed. Sometimes, highway industrial buildings, vacant supermarkets, and empty inner-city buildings are transformed into antique malls so their owners can collect rent on otherwise unused space. Such mall operators know little or nothing about the antiques business or retailing; all they are interested in is collecting rent so they can make their mortgage payment. These landlords charge rent based on the size of a booth regardless of the location of the space. Don't be fooled: some spaces are more valuable than others. Don't lease a poor booth location; you'll regret it.

How to identify the best locations within a mall

Choosing the best booth location within a mall is a matter of understanding how shoppers move within a store.

Fortunately, the subject "how shoppers move" has been well researched. In the 1970s, social scientist Paco Underhill began to videotape how customers moved through stores. In over forty years of research he compiled more than one hundred thousand hours of videotape. His aim was to improve traffic flow and increase sales. His findings revolutionized the way retail stores are laid out (grocery stores in particular) and his client list includes AT&T, Starbucks, Apple, and dozens of other first-tier retailers. Underhill's research gave rise to a new branch of social science called "retail anthropology".

Here's how most shoppers will move through your mall:

● When a shopper first enters a mall, they stop briefly to look around and let their eyes adjust to their surroundings. The area just inside the door is called the "decompression zone". Never lease a booth in this area, because traffic will walk right past you.

• Shoppers have a natural inclination to move right, look straight ahead, and avoid bending over. The best booth spaces are those that customers see without having to look right or left; i.e., at the end of aisles. As you take your inspection walk through your mall, every time you take a turn notice which booths are directly in your line of sight. Those are the best locations to have.

• Upon entry. most shoppers turn right and proceed to the far-right wall. This wall is valuable real estate. Take it if you can get it.

• On the way to the rear wall, shoppers notice displays on the right and left that are at eye level. But they won't stop to browse unless you can slow them down. For now, they are focused on the back wall (end of aisle).

• Shoppers are slowed down by reflective surfaces.

• Browsers turn left at the back wall, and continue until they hit the far-left wall. Then, they proceed down the left wall until they come to the front. Next, they will travel up and down the center aisles.

• If a main traffic lane is built into the layout of your mall, customers will unconsciously follow the lane around the store. Usually, a mall's path is a wide lane with specialty alcoves on each side. Customers stop and shop, but when they've finished browsing, they get back on the path.

•   Side caps facing the main traffic flow outsell opposite-facing side caps by a factor of five.

If you can't find a good spot along an outside wall, then these are good alternate choices:

•   A booth at the intersection of connecting aisles

•   A booth near the restrooms or snack bar. I know a mall dealer who successfully sold items displayed in the restrooms, and he got the space for free by agreeing to clean the area once a week (the mall had to clean them in-between his visits).

•   If you can't find space in any of the above areas, try to locate your booth near dealers who carry items like yours. A concentration of similar items attracts shoppers.

Finding the right spot to set up your booth is like finding the right spot to build a house. The location might look good, but you still must put a pencil to paper and draw up some plans. You would never think of buying some lumber and roofing and jumping right into building without a plan. The house would fall, for sure.

Neither should you consider just buying inventory and throwing up a few displays in your booth. Just as a poorly executed house would fall, a poorly executed business will fail. Next, let's have a look at what you can do to plan for your booth's success.

Chapter Four: Staying Profitable

Once you've found a suitable space, you're almost ready to sign a lease and set up shop. I say "almost" because at this point you haven't a clue whether you can make a profit.

If you collected the mall's sales stats you should be able to assess your ability to make a profit. In theory, making a profit is easy: Your income must be greater that your expenses. In practice, though, profits alone won't keep your business going: You also need cash. I'm sure you remember from our introduction The Profit Trap, that profits and cash are not always the same thing.

Some booths lose money in their first year. Some never make a profit. But an antique mall booth is small enough that with a wee bit of financial planning a new dealer can turn a profit within the first ninety days. But, the time to plan for profitability is before you sign a lease. Once you sign a lease, you're committed to the enterprise, profitable or not.

You can plan for profitability if you learn and apply the following four basic formulas. Yes, this is "business math", but it's the kind of business math that even a third grader can do.

- Net Sales minus Cost of Goods Sold equals Gross Profit

- Gross Profit minus Expenses equals Net Profit

- Net Profit minus Taxes equals Discretionary Cash

- Discretionary Cash minus Re-Investment equals Spendable Cash

Ultimately, your goal is to have lots of spendable cash. Spendable cash is yours to keep; it's your vacation money or new car money or mad money. It's the reason you went into business. A steady stream of spendable cash will put a smile on your face.

The above terms will come up often in your business dealings, so let me explain each one and give you a few examples. Then, we'll explore how using these formulas can help you stay profitable.

Net Sales minus Cost of Goods Sold equals Gross Profit

Net Sales is the sum of all sales from whatever venues you sell from: malls, online, shows, etc., less any returns or adjustments. The Cost of Goods Sold is the amount you paid for the goods you sold. The Gross Profit that you make on sales equals the difference between the amount you paid for an item and the amount you sold it for (Net Sales minus Cost of Goods Sold equals Gross Profit).

Gross profit doesn't tell the whole story, though. If your gross profit isn't enough to pay all expenses, you lose money on every sale you make; making more sales just means you're losing more money. As a mentor once told me: "you can't lose a nickel apiece and make it up in volume". If you are making enough gross profit to pay your booth rent but not enough to cover your car expense and re-invest in inventory, you're not "breaking even"; you're losing money.

Gross Profit minus Expenses equals Net Profit

Expenses are monies that you spend to do business. Rent, advertising, gasoline, car repairs, insurance, accounting fees, etc. are expenses. Expense money is gone once you pay it; you'll never get it back. The amount that's left over once you deduct Expenses from Gross Profit is your Net Profit. (Gross Profit minus Expenses equals Net Profit). Money that you spend on things that stick around for a while (like inventory, fixtures, and displays) are investments, not expenses.

Every dollar you use to pay your bills comes from your gross profit , so the greater your gross profit, the more money you must pay bills and grow your business.

Net Profit minus Taxes equals Discretionary Cash

Net Profit is the amount that the IRS and other taxing authorities will tax you on. This is the amount that is considered the income from your business venture. Since you must plan for paying taxes, don't spend all your net profit; put some in a tax account, and make quarterly tax payments to the IRS. Otherwise, on April 15 you won't have enough money to pay your taxes. A word to the wise: don't mess with the IRS; they can make your life miserable (ask any businessman, they'll tell you). Once you've set money aside for taxes, what remains is Discretionary Cash.

Discretionary Cash minus Re-Investment equals Spendable Cash

Discretionary Cash is yours to spend however you would like. You can grow your business by re-investing your cash in inventory or fixtures, or you can keep it. It's up to you. Whatever amount is not re-invested is your Spendable Cash. Spend it wisely, or party hearty. Your call.

Let's do a little quick profit planning so you can see how the above formulas can keep you profitable.

Imagine that you are considering a one-year lease for a 10' X 10' booth space at an antique mall. You will pay the mall a monthly rent of $150 plus 10% of sales and a 3% credit card fee. The mall manager tells you that on average, similar-sized booths have revenues of $750-$1000 month. You plan on revenue of $800 month, and you assume that half your customers will pay by credit card.

For starters, you need to generate enough Gross Profit to pay your bills. Let's apply formula #1 (Sales minus Cost of Goods Sold equals Gross Profit) to your imaginary antiques booth. For this example, I'll assume that you arrive at your retail price by doubling what you paid for your merchandise.

● $800 sales minus $400 Cost of Goods Sold equals $400 Gross Profit

So far, so good, right? We have a $400 Gross Profit.

Next, let's add up our Expenses:

● $150 Rent plus $80 Mall percentage plus $12 Credit card fees plus $40 car expense (based on .40/mile, 100 miles per month) equals $282 in total expenses.

Subtracting $282 in Expenses from $400 Gross Profit leaves us enough money to pay our bills, and that's a good thing. Let's see what we've got left:

$400 Gross Profit minus $282 Expenses equals a $118 Net Profit.

We have a Net Profit that exceeds our Expenses, so we have some cash left over to "play" with. What are our options?

- Pay taxes

- Invest in inventory, etc.

- Put it in our pocket

But, $118 isn't very much money to play with. Remember, you paid $400 for the merchandise that you sold, and now you only have $118 left. Some of the $118 you wanted to set aside for taxes and you were hoping to take your spouse out to dinner at a nice restaurant. If you spend the money on taxes and dinner, you won't have enough left over to re-invest in inventory.

You can't keep this up for too long or you'll be out of business. What can you do to improve the outcome? There are two possibilities:

- Sell more

- Increase your profit margins

Selling more could give you more cash, but it's not always possible to sell more. Plus, as long you're paying the mall a percentage of your sales, they will get a piece of every sales increase that you can achieve. A better idea is to increase your profit margins (the difference between your buying price and your selling price). Increasing profit margins will allow you to hit your profit goals faster, and you won't have to pay any of the increase to the mall. Let's see what happens when sales remain at the same level, but we multiply the wholesale cost by 3 instead of 2 to arrive at our selling price (thus increasing our margin).

- $800 sales minus $267 Cost of Goods Sold (1/3 of retail) equals $533 Gross Profit

Less Expenses: $150 Rent, $80 Mall percentage, $12 Credit card fees, $40 car expense, for a total of $282 in expenses.

- $533 Gross Profit minus $282 Expenses equals $251 Net Profit.

Our Cost of Goods Sold was $267, and the Net Profit was $251. Still not ideal, but much better from a cash-flow point of view than our previous example. You can see how increasing margins will give you more money to work with. We'll discuss ways to increase profit margins in the Chapter Seven: Buy Right to Sell Right and Chapter Eight: Pricing for Profit.

Accountants calculate the above a bit differently, using a complicated formula called a "break-even analysis". A break-even analysis tells you how much you need to sell in order to break even. At this point in your business venture (you haven't signed a lease or sold your first item) using a formal break-even analysis is overkill. But once you have a better idea of what the fixed and variable costs are for your booth you may want to perform a break-even analysis. You'll find a free break-even calculator online at Good Calculators[4].

Before you commit to a signing a mall lease (or any other lease) make sure that you can generate enough gross profit to pay all your bills, and that there is enough money left over to re-invest in inventory, pay taxes, and put some cash in your pocket. If you can't do that, it's hardly worth the effort, is it?

But, if you're already committed to a lease, don't despair. I'll show you how to squeeze more cash from your inventory in Chapter Six: How to Create More Cash. In the meantime, sharpen your pencil and figure what combination of sales, margins and expenses you'll need to make a "go" of your present situation. If your situation is unworkable, perhaps you can convince your landlord to make some concessions to keep you as a tenant. Otherwise, you may be forced to liquidate your inventory to pay off your lease commitment and walk away debt-free.

If it looks like you will be profitable, then you can feel confident about signing a lease. With your location secured, we'll turn our attention to a mall dealer's single biggest investment: inventory. But first, a word of warning.

---

[4] goodcalculators.com/break-even-calculator/

Chapter Five: How Much Inventory Is Needed?

Retailers have their own pet theories about inventory levels. Some adamantly state: "you can't sell what you don't have", so they keep inventories that are both broad and deep. On the opposite end of the spectrum are dealers who like to keep their displays sparse and stock only high-end, unique items. Their mantra is "turnover, turnover, turnover".

Which approach is better?

Both big inventories and lean inventories have their strengths and weaknesses: Too much inventory ties up cash but having too little may lose sales. The important point to remember is that you're running a business, not a museum. You need enough inventory to hit your sales goals and have enough left over to keep your customers coming back for more.

For example, imagine that your sales goal for a month was $1,000. You would need at least $1,000 inventory value at retail on hand to reach that goal. But, if that's all you had then at the end of the month you wouldn't have anything left to sell, so clearly you need to have more in stock than just $1,000 worth of inventory. But how much more inventory should you have on hand to keep your business viable? And, should all inventory items be stocked at the same levels?

Let's deal with "stocking levels" first. If you stock your booth with mixed antiques—some furniture, some smalls, some art—each type will sell at a different rate. Small goods sell faster than furniture and art.

The answer to the question "how much inventory must I have" lies in a concept called "months of supply". The idea is to have enough inventory on hand to stock your booth for a certain period; how long is up to you. You can stock your booth for the next twelve months if you like, or you can stock six months ahead. Or three. Buying enough inventory to stock twelve months ahead will tie up a lot of money. And, having enough inventory to support sales for the next twelve months doesn't mean that you will sell any more this month than you would if you had less inventory.

Say that you stock a three months' supply of smalls. How much is a three-month supply? Depends on which months you're talking about. Sales of antiques and collectibles are seasonal, so you'll need more inventory in some months than you will need in others.

Let's examine the charts below to see what our stocking levels might be for a three-month supply of smalls. "Months of Supply" can be calculated in terms of dollars or the number of items (if you calculate using dollars, be consistent: either use all retail or all wholesale figures). In the example below, I calculate "months of supply" by the number of items because it's easier to grasp the concept.

Suppose you had a superb holiday season, and you almost sold out of smalls: you had just three left at the end of the year.

You plan to sell 8 in January, and you have 3. How many more do you need to buy to hit your sales plan? Most people would say 5. They would be wrong.

Month	Sales Plan	Ending Inv	Beginning Inv	Open to Buy
January	8		3	5?

If you have 3 in stock, buy 5 more and then sell 8, how many will you have left? That's right: none. What happens if a busload of tourists pulls into your mall and you don't have any smalls to sell? You'll lose money, that's what. So, you need to buy more than just 5 so you won't miss any sales in February. Here's the formula for how to plan your purchases so you don't miss any sales, but don't buy too much inventory:

(Sales plus Ending Inventory) minus Beginning Inventory equals Open-to-Buy

Here's how to apply this:

1. If you will sell 8 in January but have only 3 in stock, you need to buy 5 more to hit your January sales plan. But if you're stocking an additional 90 days ahead, you also need to buy what you need for February, March, and April.
2. Total the number of units you want to sell in the next 90 days: 12 in February 8 in March, and 10 in April, for a total of 30.
3. To sell 30 in February, March, and April, you must have 30 on hand at the end of January. You have a shortfall of 5 already, so if you will meet your sales plan you need to buy 35 smalls in January. The difference between what you have (3) and what you need (35) is called "Open-to-Buy". To stay on-plan, you are open-to-buy 35 smalls.

Let's continue analyzing our chart:

Month	Sales Plan	Ending Inv	Beginning Inv	Open to Buy
January	8	30	3	35
February	12	36	30	18
March	8	52	36	24
April	10		52	
May	18			
June	24			

In February, we plan to sell 12 smalls (Sales Plan). We have 30 left over from January (Ending Inv.). At the end of February, we want to have 36 on-hand (Ending Inv.). How do we know that we want to have 36 on hand at the end of February? Because we looked ahead to March, April and May and added up the number of smalls we intend to sell in those months (because we're planning for a three-month supply of smalls). To have 36 on-hand at the end of February we must buy 18. The ending inventory for one month is always the beginning inventory for the next month.

In March, we plan to sell just 8 because traffic drops off in cold, snowy March (or at least it does around here). We have 36 left over from February. But because we're coming into the selling season we want to have a good selection of inventory on-hand on the first of April. To keep a 3 month supply of smalls on hand, we should buy another 24 pieces in March. And so on throughout the year.

The best way to get a "feel" for this process is to sit with a pencil, paper, and calculator and keep running the numbers until you have an "A-HA" moment. Then, you'll never forget the process. After a while, all you must do is look at your booth to predict how much you will need to buy.

Here's a five-step process for doing your own plan:

Step #1: Draw a 5-column across X 13-row down matrix (1 row for each month).

Step #2: Enter the planned sales for each month.

Step #3: Enter your ending inventory targets according to the months of supply you want.

Step #4: Enter the beginning inventory for each month. This is the easiest step of all, because the beginning inventory for one month is always the ending inventory for the previous month. Just slide the numbers over and you're "good to go".

Step #5: Now just do the arithmetic: **(Sales plus Ending Inventory) minus Beginning Inventory equals Open to Buy.**

At the end of each month, enter your actual ending inventory numbers so you can stay on-plan. If you're using a spreadsheet, changing the current month's numbers to match reality will update all the other numbers.

You will need to look ahead three months (or whatever interval you have decided on) and buy enough inventory to keep your shelves stocked for the next period. At the end of the month, according to your sales plan, you will be "open to buy" a certain amount of new inventory

Antique mall dealers often get into trouble by willy-nilly buying inventory giving no thought to what they need to have. Too much inventory leads to crowded displays, low cash reserves, and unnecessary expenses (like renting storage space to hold excess inventory, for example).

Does planning for months-of-supply mean that if you find a great deal on a unique item when you are not open-to-buy that you should pass on the purchase? Of course not. If you find something that's a great deal that will make you a nice profit then buy it. What it means, however, is that you are now over-inventoried according your plan. To stay on track, you should mark down a few items to reduce your inventory level. Don't just keep accumulating inventory. If you do, you'll wake up one morning and find that you are drowning in inventory and have no cash to pay your bills or to buy anything new. Such a circumstance is called "inventory rich and cash poor". Happens all the time; don't let it happen to you.

My opinion is that having a three to six-month supply of inventory on hand is all you need. I've concluded that by thinking like a customer. If customers returning to your booth see the same inventory items over and over, they will eventually stop browsing your booth. You must keep your inventory small enough that you can continually buy and display new items; otherwise, your customers will get bored with what you have. Stocking a twelve-month supply means that your regular visitors will keep seeing the same items over and over.

How do you determine how many items you need, when you set your budget according to dollars?

Once you've decided how much inventory you need to carry in terms of gross dollars, translate this amount into the number of items you will need to have in inventory, and the price points at which they will sell.

For example, let's say that your monthly sales goal is $1,000. If your specialty is bottles, and your average bottle price is $10, you must make 100 sales (more or less) a month to reach your $1,000 goal. Is this do-able in your mall? Will the mall traffic support selling 100 bottles every month? Will you be able to find antique bottles in sufficient quantity to restock your inventory, month after month, year after year? These are questions that you should consider when developing your inventory strategy.

If all you stocked is high-end collectible bottles with an average sale price of $200 then you'd only have to sell 5 bottles to hit your goal.

Smart retailers know that more goods are sold at low prices than are sold at high prices. Some customers who visit your booth may spend $300-$400 on a bottle, but most will not. You'll capture more customers and create more future business by offering a range of price points. You won't get any new customers interested in collecting bottles if all you offer is high priced bottles. To develop new business, offer some bottles at entry-level prices. Until you have made enough sales to track your most profitable price points, offer 30% of your inventory at a low price point, 50% in the mid-range, and 20%

high-end. Depending on what type of merchandise you're selling "low" might be several thousand dollars, so adapt your prices according to your research.

Is Buy Low, Sell High for Amateurs?

If you've followed along so far, you probably have a good feel for how much inventory you'll need to stock your booth. Now, let's put to rest another myth common among antique dealers. Here it is:

Always buy low and sell high.

The problem with this myth is the word "always". As a general operating principle, "buy low and sell high" is right on the money. But sometimes dealers get so caught up in selling items for more than they paid for them, that they lose track of the bigger profit picture. To use one platitude to describe another, such dealers "can't see the forest for the trees".

I'm not suggesting that you take a loss on your "choice" inventory items; profit must come from somewhere. But we all have items in our inventory that aren't selling. Some of us have a LOT of inventory items that aren't selling. We all make buying mistakes, no matter how careful we are. We buy the wrong item, or we pay too much for an item. Over time, these buying mistakes collect like silt in a riverbed: a half-dozen items or more accumulate every month, and eventually we're awash in dead inventory. Our retail ship won't float because it's stuck on a financial sandbar. Too much silt, too much dead inventory. We sell newer items while the old, dead inventory sits there, takes up space, and costs us more money to hold.

The way to stay ahead of dead stock is to visualize your inventory as an organic whole rather than a collection of individual items. Don't micro-manage your inventory. Think of your inventory as if it's a stock portfolio. Like a stock portfolio, your inventory is an investment; in fact, it's the biggest investment that a retailer has. And, it's the hardest working investment. Your inventory must pay all your expenses plus provide enough money for re-stocking and provide your "mad money". You wouldn't keep an employee around who wasn't pulling his weight; why keep an item in inventory that isn't pulling its weight?

Individual stocks in a portfolio rise and fall in value. At the end of a year, it is the performance of the portfolio that makes money or loses money. Likewise, it's the performance of your inventory portfolio that makes you money and keeps your customers coming back. Don't obsess over individual items.

Sometimes selling an item for less than you paid for it will free up cash so you can buy a more saleable item. I'm sure you'll sell some items for 3x, 5x, 10x, or 15 times what you paid. Shouldn't you also be willing to take a loss on a few items? Win some, lose some. Over the course of a year, individual items in your inventory should be evaluated. Are you getting an adequate return on your investment, or not? You buy inventory for just one reason: to turn it into cash. If an investment isn't giving you an adequate return, then sell it at a loss so that new investments can be made.

At the end of the year, the performance of your inventory is a major factor in profitability. Consider how the IRS requires you to report your inventory. Here's the relevant section of the IRS Schedule C:

Part III   Cost of Goods Sold (see instructions)

33	Method(s) used to value closing inventory: a ☐ Cost b ☐ Lower of cost or market c ☐ Other (attach explanation)	
34	Was there any change in determining quantities, costs, or valuations between opening and closing inventory? If "Yes," attach explanation . . . . ☐ Yes ☐ No	
35	Inventory at beginning of year. If different from last year's closing inventory, attach explanation . .	35
36	Purchases less cost of items withdrawn for personal use	36
37	Cost of labor. Do not include any amounts paid to yourself	37
38	Materials and supplies	38
39	Other costs	39
40	Add lines 35 through 39	40
41	Inventory at end of year	41
42	Cost of goods sold. Subtract line 41 from line 40. Enter the result here and on line 4 . . .	42

At tax time, the cost of goods sold comes down to (starting inventory plus purchases minus ending inventory). No consideration is given to individual items. Dealers would do well to perceive their inventory the same way the IRS does: as an organic whole.

Coming to terms with this concept can be tough. I once had a dealer say to me "I just have a gut feeling that if I always sell for more than I paid that everything will work out".

That's not surprising. There is a psychological basis for antique dealers wanting to hang on to their inventory: It's called "loss aversion". Loss aversion isn't solely about losing money on an item; it's a psychological driver that affects other aspects of our lives as well. In terms of buying and selling, the essence of loss aversion is that once something is in your possession and you own it, it increases in value to you. We don't like losing something once we own it. The loss aversion we experience when we refuse to sell an item for less than we paid for it (even a very old item) is explained in part by a classroom exercise that is regularly conducted by Eric Johnson of the Columbia University School of Business:

In the exercise, Professor Johnson divides his class into two groups. The first group is shown a coffee mug and asked how much they would pay for it. They never possess the coffee mug. Most of the time the students say that they would pay around $4.00 for the mug. In the second group, each student is given a coffee mug to keep that is identical to the mug shown to the first group. Then, they are asked how much they would sell it for. The members of the "selling" group want, on average, about $8.00 each for their mugs. Remember, this is a mug they got for free. The second group did not know of the price set by the first group; they simply wanted $8 before they would part with their mugs. The mug was more valuable to them because they owned it.

Year after year, professor Johnson's experiment shows the same result: that there is a considerable difference between how much we will pay for an item and how much we would sell it for once we own it.

And that's the way we feel about the items in our inventory, isn't it? We spent time digging through estate sales and yard sales and bidding at auctions to come up with our inventory items. Money aside, we have invested our time and effort into acquiring these items. It's tough to recognize that we may have made a mistake, and our inclination is to hold the item until the market turns around or the right buyer walks in. To stay profitable, keep your inventory fresh and your customers happy, don't micro-manage. Rather, view your inventory as an organic whole.

When you come to recognize that some items need to be marked down and moved out, do so methodically.

Having made these points, allow me to offer a few suggestions gained from over 40 years of owning retail stores:

• Your inventory is your best marketing tool. What you have on display and how your stock is displayed says a lot about your business. You want your booth to stop mall browsers in their tracks and have them declare "Wow! Look at this!"

• You'll never be entirely satisfied with what you have in stock. You'll worry that you're missing sales. That's normal. As I've said before, you're running a business not a museum. Invest wisely in your inventory and your inventory will provide you with a nice profit.

• Don't buy stock just to fill up the space you have. Instead, get creative with your displays. If you run out of space, don't start renting storage space because storage space can be addicting. If you have too much inventory (and you are profitable and have good cash flow at your current location) then consider renting a booth at another mall. Customers can't buy what you have stored away; keep everything displayed.

• Customers want choices. Offer multiples of the same item and price them high, medium, and low.

Inventory planning presupposes that you have made a sales plan for the year. If you haven't, first make a sales plan and then make an inventory plan.

Chapter Six: How to Create More Cash

In the Introduction, we discussed the Profit Trap. We identified the Profit Trap as being your inventory and noted how inventory can disguise profits and suck up cash. In this chapter, we'll talk about how to release the cash that's locked up in your inventory.

As we get started some of you will say: "Well, getting more cash from inventory is easy; just sell more". And they would be right, to a point. But how much more can you sell? All retail stores eventually hit a sales ceiling that's tough to penetrate. In some years your sales are a little higher than average and in other years sales are down a bit. But mostly you stay pretty much in the same range year after year. Maybe you have all the market share you're likely to get in your mall because there is not enough traffic to support higher sales.

Some of you might point out that raising prices will create more cash. Maybe it will; but raising prices may also result in some lost sales. How about paying less for your resale merchandise? Won't that also create more cash? It will; if your retail prices stay put.

Chances are, you're already doing these things to get more cash out of your inventory but still have cash flow problems. Taken together, the tactics mentioned won't, by themselves, fix a cash problem.

But I have some good news for you: there's a way to improve the return on your inventory investment and free up cash without increasing sales, raising prices, or "buying better". That way is to focus on GMROI, or Gross Margin Return on Inventory Investment. Focusing on GMROI, simply put, is to adjust your inventory levels, prices, margins, and sales to create the amount of cash that you need to pay all of your expenses, grow your business, and have enough money left over to pay yourself handsomely.

Once you understand GMROI, you may discover that:

- You can generate higher profits from fewer sales

- You can make more money with reduced margins

- You need less inventory to hit your sales goals

- You have more cash available to reduce debt and grow your business

The GMROI calculation answers the question "how much money do I get back for every dollar I invest in inventory"? The Gross Profit (or Gross Margin) that is created when you make sales needs to provide enough money to operate and grow your business and make a profit. It makes sense to squeeze all the dollars you can from your inventory. GMROI allows you to discover ways to do this without raising sales or prices.

The two key factors in GMROI are the amount of your inventory investment, and the amount of your Gross Margin. You probably are already familiar with these numbers, but you might not be familiar with these terms in this context. So that everyone reading this chapter can keep up, let me backtrack just a little and review these two terms before moving on.

When you start in business, you use some of your cash to buy inventory. Your intention is to sell the inventory for more than you paid for it and use some of the resulting income to buy more inventory and some of it to pay your operating expenses. On your income statement, your sales revenue shows up as Sales, and the amount you paid for your inventory displays as Cost of Goods Sold (COGS). You'll recall from our discussion in Chapter Four: Staying Profitable that the difference between Sales and Cost of Goods Sold is your Gross Profit.

Here's how to calculate your GMROI, in three easy steps, using your annual Gross Profit (in dollars) and your average Inventory @cost:

Step # 1: Calculate Gross Profit dollars. The formula is: Sales minus Cost of Goods Sold equals Gross Profit. For example, (keeping the numbers simple for the sake of the example) if your total sales for the year were $20,000 and your Cost of Goods Sold was $10,000, then $20,000 minus $10,000 equals $10,000. Your Gross Profit is $10,000.

Step #2: Calculate Average Inventory at Cost. To figure your average inventory for a year, add up your ending inventories (at wholesale cost) for each month of the year, plus the ending inventory (at cost) for the previous year. Then, to get the average, divide the total of those inventories by 13, the number of inventories in the sum. Let's assume, again keeping it simple, that the sum of all those inventories (including last year's fiscal year-end) was $120,000. Then, using the formula, $120,000 divided by 13 equals $9,320.

Step #3: Calculate GMROI. Here's the formula: Annual Gross Margin Dollars ($10,000) divided by Average Inventory at Cost ($9,230) equals GMROI.

So, $100,000 divided by $100,000 equals 1.08.

"So what?" you say. What does that tell me? What it tells you is that for every dollar you have invested in inventory you are getting a dollar and eight cents back to pay all your expenses and buy new inventory.

No one can maintain a business at that level; roughly a dollar back for every dollar spent on inventory will barely give you enough money to replace the inventory, much less pay the bills. But, by rounding down the $1.08 to $1 (just to keep the math simple) and keeping Sales and Gross Margin the same, let's see what happens to GMROI when the amount of dead inventory we have continues to rise, and our average inventory goes up to $12,500:

- Sales of $20,000 minus COGS of $10,000 equals $10,000 Gross Profit.

- $10,000 Gross Profit divided by $12,500 Average Inventory equals 0.80.

Your inventory went up by $3,270. Since you have more money invested inventory and your sales and margins have remained the same, the return on your inventory investment went down to eighty cents for every dollar invested. The return on your inventory investment just got worse.

Let's take one more look at the effect of an inventory increase, bringing our inventory level up to $15,000:

- Sales of $20,000 minus COGS: $10,000 equals $10,000 Gross Profit.

- $10,000 Gross Margin divided by $15,000 Average Inventory equals 0.68.

Your inventory went up by an additional $2,500, and since your sales and margins didn't change the return on your inventory investment went down to sixty-eight cents for every dollar invested. You're losing money, big-time.

Now let's reduce your inventory instead of increasing it and see what happens. Suppose that your inventory goes down to $5,000 (which can happen if you use an open-to-buy system), while the same margins and sales levels are maintained:

- Sales of $20,000 minus COGS $10,000 equals $10,000 Gross Profit.

- $10,000 Gross Margin divided by $5,000 Average Inventory equals 2.0.

Cut your inventory in half, and your GMROI doubles to $2 for every dollar invested. Wall Street bankers would kill for that return.

Not only are you getting a better return on your inventory investment, you just freed up almost $5,000 in cash. Makes sense, doesn't it? Your sales revenue has remained the same, and the cost of the merchandise that you sold remained the same. The only difference is that you are turning your inventory over faster. You no longer carry a twelve-month supply of inventory; you carry a six-month supply. Money that would have gone into maintaining a high inventory level can now be used to pay your bills.

Does a three-to-six-month supply of inventory sound like too little for you? It's not, really. Industry benchmarks for used merchandise dealers show that they routinely turn their inventory four times per year; in other words, they sell from a three-month supply of inventory. Some retailers (grocery stores, for example) turn their inventories twelve times a year or more, varying by department.

The important point is to know that by adjusting your inventory levels you can get a better return on your inventory investment (everything else being equal), and free up cash to use for other purposes. Experiment with your sales, margins, and inventory turns on a spreadsheet to see what combination works best in your situation.

Know that GMROI is not a magic wand that will fix a cash flow problem. Rather, it is a tool that gives insight into how certain variables work together to give the best return on your inventory investment. GMROI calculations allow you to manipulate those variables so you can see what must be done to reach your objectives. Like any tool, its effectiveness will depend on how well you use it. Using it well requires thoughtfulness on your part.

The biggest "cash trap" that small retailers have is their inventory. GMROI is one tool that can be used to keep the cash flowing and your business growing.

Chapter Seven: Buy Right to Sell Right

You know that the essence of retailing is buy low, sell high. That's true. What's unclear in this pithy statement is just how low is low and how high is high enough to pay all the bills and make a profit.

Historically, buying antiques and collectibles for resale was a crapshoot. Dealers made purchases based on how well they knew their customers' buying habits and whatever "good deals" they could find. If a dealer found an item they thought would sell in their store that they could mark-up to two or three times, then they would buy it if they could afford it. Many of today's dealers still use this method.

What dealers could never know for sure when they made a purchase in that manner was how many similar items were for sale around town and what competitive dealers were charging for those items. Sure, dealers were often guilty of sneaking a peek at prices in a competitor's store, but they could only get away with that for so long. Once your face is known around town it's difficult to sneak into a competitor's store to check out their prices.

Even when a dealer knew a competitor's prices, she could never know how many of her customers walked away from an item because the price was too high.

In years past dealers could not determine the supply of an item, the demand for an item, or the "right price" for any item they wanted to buy before they shelled out cash and put it in their store. It would take a dealer many years to gain enough experience buying and selling to guess what his profit would be on any individual sale.

Fortunately, buying inventory for resale is a lot easier for today's dealers (if they do it right). Here are five tips for buying right so you can sell right. Whenever you find an item that looks like it's a good buy, do the following:

• First ask yourself if the item is a good fit for your booth. What separates your booth from others in your mall is primarily the quality, categories, and prices of your merchandise. There are other things as well—like merchandising, location, and access to information—but those topics we cover in other chapters. For now, let's stick to the subject of buying right. Whatever you do, don't buy something just because it's a good deal or because you have space to fill. Your inventory makes a strong statement about your booth, so fill your shelves with profitable items that you are proud to offer.

• Is there a demand for this item? No matter how good a "deal" you might believe an item to be, if there is no demand for the item then you shouldn't buy it. Even "free" items take up space and, over time, cost you money. That's why auctioneers are picky about what they take on consignment: a lot of money can be spent moving things around, tagging, displaying, and selling. Free is rarely free; cheap is rarely cheap. If you take items on consignment, pay attention to this point. You're not in the storage business, you're a retailer. Make sure that there is a demand for what you offer for sale. Some say that demand can be created with clever marketing. I say let someone else market those items. For a good retail buyer, such items are nothing but a distraction.

• How many of these (or similar) items are offered for sale? It no longer matters that you might be the only store in your town with a particular item in inventory because you are also competing with every online seller. Unless you have a competitive advantage (like price or condition) don't buy items which are in good supply because you won't get a good price for them.

• What are the high and low selling prices for the item you're interested in? Don't count on getting the higher price when you re-sell it. Buy at a price that will keep you profitable even if you can only achieve a lower price.

Ultimately, it's not a good buy if it's not a good sell. Know how you intend to sell an item before you buy it.

There are online tools that can be used to research the supply and demand for a wide variety of items. To use these tools, you will need a smartphone or tablet and an account with the service you intend to use. Don't scout for inventory without these tools; you will be at a huge disadvantage if you do. Whenever you find an item you think is a good fit for your store, your first move should be to look it up on eBay. If you know the name and manufacturer of the item start with a specific search. If you don't know the name and manufacturer, start by using an "all categories" search to be sure you're categorizing the item in the same fashion that sellers are. If you can't find your specific item, it may be helpful to find similar items in the same category.

When your search results display, look in eBay's left sidebar; you will see a heading that reads "Show Only"; click the box that says "Completed Listings". The search results will then display unsold (in red) and sold (in green) items that match your search criteria. The items listed will tell you:

- How many items like yours are being offered for sale and

- How many of them sold

In addition, you will discover which prices produced sales and which prices didn't produce sales. The ratio of sold to unsold items is also important; ideally, you want there to be more demand (green prices) than supply (red prices). All other things being equal, when there is more demand than supply prices will go up; and when the supply is greater than the demand prices will go down.

eBay is not the only online source for researching your items. For price research I use Terapeak, WorthPoint, Kovels, and Heritage Auctions. To determine supply and demand, Terapeak is easiest to use, but eBay is free.

From time to time websites will pop up that claim to access eBay to provide you with supply and demand information. If you find one you like, use it. Over the years I've found that such sites come and go, so I always return to eBay.

Another way to ballpark what the demand might be for an item is to use the Google Keyword Planner to determine search volume for a particular item.

Knowing what the demand is for an item you are considering and knowing the prices that similar items bring will enable you to take an educated guess at how long the item might sit in your booth and what price it might bring when you sell it. Armed with such information, you'll be able to better determine what you will pay for an item, and how you should price it. Pricing your items is our next topic.

Chapter Eight: Pricing for Profit

Pricing your goods for sale is more art than science, but over the years generations of retailers have devised a few pricing tactics that will keep your inventory moving off the shelf. Here are a few of the more popular tactics:

Keystone pricing is the most common method of pricing antiques. "Keystoning" occurs when you take the price you pay for an inventory item and double or triple it to hit your retail price. If you pay $30 for an antique widget, you double it to get a retail price of $60. The keystone is "2X", meaning "two times the (wholesale price).

Antique dealers are one of the few remaining retail businesses that can use keystoning effectively. Stores that sell commoditized goods—from Wal-Mart to the corner convenience store—are so discount-oriented and competitive that keystone pricing doesn't work for them. Often, their markups are 10% or 20% over wholesale. Fortunately, keystoning still works great for the antiques business.

Many antique and vintage dealers use a 2X keystone, but keystone doesn't always have to be 2X. I know an online seller who, before he decides what to pay for an item, checks the item online and never pays over 1/3 of its average selling price. In other words, he sells for approximately three times what he pays. His "keystone" number is 3X. His bottom line isn't always three time what he pays, because he sometimes puts items on sale. Overall, though, he averages better than double what he pays, which is good. Better to start high and come down. You can always lower prices, but rarely can you raise them.

The strength of keystoning is that it's easy to use, and the keystone calculation can be done quickly in your head when you're at an auction or negotiating a price at an estate sale.

Sometimes, though, keystoning can cause a retail price that's too low. For example, let's say that you're browsing through a box of 8-track tapes at a garage sale and find a quadrophonic Sinatra-Jobim tape. That's a rare tape, and collectors will pay a lot for it. The garage sale tapes you are browsing are $5 for the whole box, and you know that a mint quad version of Sinatra-Jobim is currently selling for about $4,000. Of course, you'll buy the whole box of tapes, even if most are unsaleable. But it would be foolish to use your keystone to price the tape; you'd lose money, big-time. So, don't get too stuck on keystoning. Remember that there is a market value for everything, and you should be pricing your products at their market value.

What if the market value of what you bought turns out to be less than your keystone? What if you paid $15 for an item that you could only sell for $20? Or $10? Then you didn't do your homework before you bought it; you overpaid. Regardless of what you paid for your item, it's only worth what someone will pay for it. So, should you keep it and hope the value goes up to match your price? Of course not! You made a mistake; everyone does in this business. Suck it up, price the item for what you can get for it and move it out the door. Be more careful next time.

Another time when keystoning is the wrong approach is when your keystone doesn't generate enough money to pay your bills, based on your sales level. This circumstance occurs when a business is brand-new, and sales aren't very high. You'll recall that we covered this topic in the chapter "Staying Profitable". For now, let's continue with more pricing strategies.

Benchmark pricing is when you price your goods according to what your competitors are charging. If there are other dealers in your mall offering items like yours, comparison shoppers will buy the item that offers the best value. There are two ways to ensure that you'll get the sale:

• Make sure that your item is in better condition and is offered at a matching or lower price.

• Bundle your item with one or more additional items to create a "value added" package (see Multiples Pricing below). Doing so will divert attention from the fact that your item may be more expensive (or in less desirable condition) than your competitor's item.

You see benchmark pricing a lot in commodity retailing; a good example is an ad that reads "we match competitor's coupons". Some antique dealers match their retail prices to that of similar items being offered online. That's an acceptable retail pricing strategy provided you know there's a difference between asking price and selling price. It's very instructive to check eBay's "completed listings" for an item and compare completed listings (red numbers) to sold listings (green numbers) If you don't know how to do this, review Chapter Seven: Buy Right to Sell Right.

Markup pricing: Markup is a retailing term that's often misused. It's a simple concept: starting with what you paid for a product (wholesale cost) you then "mark up" the wholesale cost by a certain percentage. Keystoning is a type of markup, but one that works with whole numbers rather than a percentage. The key word in "markup" is "UP". Starting with the wholesale cost, then you multiply UP to get your retail.

The reason I mention this is that "markup" is often confused with "margin". Margin is more correctly called "operating margin". Markup is calculated before an item is sold, and margin is calculated after an item is sold. Margin is a measure of profitability and can be calculated only after considering all the expenses of doing business are known.

For now, it's enough to know that markup and margin are not the same thing.

Psychological pricing focuses on what customers will pay for a product, rather than focusing on what the retailer needs to charge to hit his profit goals.

So far, the pricing strategies we have discussed have been formulaic: if I pay X for a product, then I should sell my product for Y. When I was first in business, that's how I operated.

Then, I had a meeting with my friend Bill, who is probably the smartest retailer I have ever known. He's a Harvard MBA, and the owner of one of the country's most successful specialty retail chains. When I told Bill that I was struggling to make ends meet, the first thing he ask me was how I arrived at my retail prices. I told him I used various formulas involving markup from cost.

He then told me something that took me weeks to sort out and understand; something I've never forgotten. He said: "What you pay for a product has absolutely nothing to do with how much you charge for it".

As it turns out, Bill was right. Consumers will pay what they believe to be a fair price for a product, and that price has nothing to do with what it costs you to provide the product. From a standpoint of production cost alone, a Starbucks latte should retail for less than twenty-five cents and digital text messages should cost about 1 cent per 100,000 texts. They don't. In my neighborhood, a tall Starbucks latte costs $4. My phone plan charges $5 for 1,000 text messages. Off-plan, text messages cost .25 each. Why? Because that's how much consumers will pay. They may not like it, but they pay it.

Psychological pricing is based on two well-proven principles:

• Consumers have no idea what products should cost; they can only determine relative value. This is good news for antiques and art dealers, because variables such as quality, condition, rarity, etc. make feature-by-feature comparison shopping difficult. Consumers are forced to compare similar items, because an exact match can seldom be found.

• The more money you ask for, the more you get (on average).

With those two principles in mind, here are a few psychological pricing techniques:

Anchoring is the technique of providing a high number as a point of comparison. Consumers love a choice; that's why it's called "shopping". They want to compare items to find the best value. Providing a high price to anchor their comparison allows you to charge—and get—a higher price for similar goods. For example, if you have three hurricane lamps priced at $129, $89, and $69, the $129 price provides a mental "anchor" for a customer's comparison. They think: "Sometimes hurricane lamps cost $129". Most customers would then choose the mid-priced $89 lamp; but if you price the $129 lamp at $99 it will appear to be the better value and will be the lamp you are likely to sell. You won't necessarily be taking a lower margin on the $99 lamp, either. Perhaps you got a better deal on it when you bought it, or maybe you bought all three at an estate sale as a "3-fer". Or, if the $89 lamp appears "just as good as" the $99 lamp, the $89 lamp might seem to be the better bargain. "Anchor pricing" is all a matter of perception (the shoppers).

Charm pricing: Research has confirmed that prices ending in the numbers 9, 7, or 8, are effective, and their effectiveness has nothing to do with being a few cents cheaper. Also notable is the concept of "SALE". Every retailer has them, but proper signage is critical. The placement of the word "SALE" on a sign in combination with effective anchor and charm prices can mean the difference between a consumer seeing an item or not seeing it.

Psychological pricing is not about value based on what you paid for an item when you bought it. It's about understanding how much a consumer will pay, and then getting them to pay that amount. On average, you'll make more money if you price your products this way. But, you have to live with the corollary as well: when customers are only willing to pay less than what you are asking—and you need to move the item—you sometimes have to sell for less.

Discount Pricing: see Chapter Nine: When to Take Markdowns.

Multiples pricing is a strategy whereby you offer groups of items for one price, like "3 for $1". This strategy works well when you are overstocked on certain items and want to sell them off in quantities to reduce your inventory level. Some collectibles—like vinyl records, postcards, and other small goods—lend themselves well to this strategy. Multiples pricing offers you the opportunity to mix some slow-moving inventory in with your more desirable inventory and get a good average markup on the group.

Loss leader pricing is just what it sounds like: selling some items at less than you paid for them. Many retailers use such a tactic to move dead inventory while simultaneously attracting new customers, clearing shelf space, and creating some cash flow.

The key to effective loss leader pricing is to display your profitable items next to the loss-leader items in order to sell those, too. Only use loss leaders when it's clear that the lost profits can be offset by the sales of other products.

Prestige Pricing is all about synergy. Synergy occurs when your inventory, merchandising, and location work together to give customers the impression that you offer "nothing but the best". When these three components work together, you can charge top-dollar prices. The strategy behind prestige pricing is tied more to your image than the comparative quality of your products. Your products can't be cheap or fraudulently misrepresented; but, by giving your merchandise an elite look and tagging it with a high price, its implied value will rise. This pricing aims to capitalize on buyers' notions that one brand's high-priced item is superior in quality to a similar item that could be purchased for less elsewhere. Customers who shop in Prestige malls have higher-than-average disposable income and rarely bicker over price. To well-heeled customers, bickering over a few dollars is demeaning, so they don't do it. Many famous brands of automobiles, clothing, and other consumer goods use this method as a marketing strategy.

For day-to-day operations, find an appropriate keystone for your retail prices, leaving yourself room to come down in price if you need to. Mix & match the other pricing strategies according to what inventory items you need to move out the door. Keep records of all the price changes you make to inventory items (on your computer, so the information can be analyzed) and over time you will develop a "feel" for what needs to be done to keep your inventory healthy and profitable.

Chapter Nine: When to Take Mark-Downs

It happens every year between Christmas and New Years' Day: Main Street retailers mark down their inventory and hold "After Christmas" sales. Some consumers look for these sales and postpone a portion of their Christmas buying until after Christmas. Most consumers, however, don't wait until after Christmas to buy gifts. Come Christmas morning, they want presents under the tree, and the only way to make that happen is to make their purchases before Christmas.

Professional retailers (read: major chain stores) don't wait until after Christmas to offer their goods for sale; they offer special discounts on some (or much) of their merchandise before Christmas. Why? The answer is simple: because that's when most people are shopping. What's the point of marking down inventory when there won't be many shoppers in your store?

A primary difference between professionally managed retail stores and mom-and-pop stores is that the pros know when to mark down inventory, what inventory should be marked down, and how much of a markdown to take on each item. And, they do so in a way that improves, rather than worsens, the bottom line.

So, when is the best time to take markdowns, which merchandise should be marked down, how much should the markdowns be, and how often should the same merchandise be marked down? The answers to these questions can be found in the aisles of the national chain stores. Let's consider some of the above questions, and perhaps a few others along the way:

The first step to take in considering markdowns is to get your "head on straight" regarding your inventory. You purchased inventory for one reason, and that's to resell it at a profit. If an item is not selling - or if you can't get the price you want for it - mark it down. In the antique business, you can either be a collector or you can be a dealer, but you can't be both at the same time (at least within the walls of your booth). We in the antique business spend a lot of time gaining expertise about our specialty. We scout for inventory, and we are often reluctant to let an item go for less money than we think it should bring. Don't get too attached to your products; remember, you're stocking a store, not a museum. Pro retailers love their products, but only for their sales.

Don't take markdowns personally; do what needs to be done. Consider markdowns to be (in baseball terms) a bunt. Why do coaches call for a batter to bunt? To move a runner into scoring position. The coach knows beforehand that the bunting batter will likely be thrown out at first base, but it's the price he pays for moving a runner into scoring position. It's called a "sacrifice" play. When you take mark downs, you are sacrificing some of your inventory to free up cash to buy items that will sell faster or perhaps be more profitable. In the end, you'll put your business in a better position by taking markdowns.

So, which items in your inventory should be marked down? Some items you will only mark down during a mall-wide sale. But your excess inventory should be marked down on a regular and consistent basis.

How do you know what inventory is excess? Pro retailers say that any inventory that is older than "one turn" is excess. You'll find a discussion of inventory turns in Chapter Five: How Much Inventory Is Needed?, but for this discussion let me say that whenever a pro retailer buys an item for resale, he expects to have it sold by a certain date. If it doesn't sell by that date, then it's excess inventory.

In the antique and vintage trades, there are two types of excess inventory: good excess and bad excess. Both good and bad excess inventory should be evaluated in terms of "the law of supply and demand". You remember the law of supply and demand, right? It states that all other things being equal, the greater the supply of an item, the lower its' price will be. Conversely, the lower the supply of an item the higher its' price will be.

Let's apply this law to "good excess" inventory. Say you bought an estate that had hundreds of 1950s-era ceramic knick-knacks. Can you sell those? Sure you can. You'll get an initial sales bump from people who collect them, but once they've seen everything you've got and bought everything they want to collect; you won't sell any more. So, there's a limit to how many of those items you will sell in your booth. Also, having too many knick-knacks sitting on your shelf may also lower the average price you can get; too much supply equals lower prices.

When a situation like that presents itself, you must decide how many ceramic knick-knacks you think you can sell, and in what period of time. Anything over that number is excess inventory. There's nothing wrong with the items themselves; they're perfectly good. There are just too many of them. So, sell them at a low price to someone who is not a competitor; as a mixed lot on eBay, for example. Better yet—if you can—don't buy so many in the first place.

Bad excess inventory is easy to spot. Those are items that may be too worn to attract attention, or items that are commonly found that no one wants. Beanie Babies, for example. Once a hot collectible, they now fill closets all over America. Other "bad excess" inventory consists of items gained when you bought an estate and "took the good with the bad". These are items that nobody wants; there is no demand for these products. Low demand equals low price, no demand equals worthless. Bad excess inventory is like having dirty oil in your car: it gums up the engine and affects the performance of the entire car. Bad excess inventory is, well, BAD. Get rid of it as quickly as possible.

When is the best time to markdown inventory? And how often should it be marked down? The short answer is "sooner rather than later". The longer answer is that you should put each item in your inventory on a markdown schedule when you acquire it. If you start with a healthy markup, mark items down once they have been in your booth for 90 days, and then at least every 30 days thereafter. You get to decide what the mark-down schedule should be; it's your business and you know your business better than anyone else. If you have set your inventory plan (as discussed in Chapter Five: How Much Inventory Is Needed) for two turns a year, then an item you bought on Feb 1 should be sold no later than July 1. Expecting 4th of July shoppers? Good! Then you should have customers in your store to see your marked-down items. Don't chicken out: take the mark-downs when they need to be taken. Love your products but if they haven't sold within the allotted time mark them down and SELL THEM.

Marking down inventory won't do you any good if customers don't see the item. Out of sight equals no sale. So, besides marking down your prices you should take some extra steps to see that the inventory is sold. For tips on how to display your marked-down inventory (and everything else in your booth) see Chapter Ten: Selling and Merchandising.

What if you do all these things and still can't sell the items you want to move? Give them away. Giving away inventory may sound extreme but doing so may improve your cash flow. Here's how:

You'll recall that for tax purposes, your Cost of Goods Sold is calculated as follows:

(Beginning Inventory plus Purchases) minus Ending Inventory equals Cost of Goods Sold.

When you give away your unsaleable inventory, you decrease your ending inventory, which raises your Cost of Goods Sold. An increase in COGS results in lower profit (on paper). In reality, your cash hasn't suffered and since you have lower profits, you'll pay less taxes on the profits, and less personal property taxes on your remaining inventory. But please: don't take my word for it. Discuss all tax matters with your tax advisor.

Chapter Ten: Selling and Merchandising

When I was in elementary school (back in the days of yore), my classmates and I took part in an exercise called "Show and Tell". You may have taken part in this, too: each morning, a student would stand in front of the class, show a favorite or interesting object, and tell about it.

I've often described the selling that occurs in an antique mall as "show and tell without the tell". Mostly, booth displays just sit there passively while shoppers browse. Rarely is there anyone available in an antique mall to answer questions, provide insight, or make a sale. Malls don't hire sales staff; they hire clerks to keep the place straight and work the register. Some malls operate using volunteer workers, but most are dealers who are more interested in selling their goods than your goods.

Believe it or not, the lack of sales effort at an antique mall can work to your advantage, if you'll do the following:

• Create displays that will cause shoppers to slow down and investigate your booth. Remember our discussion in Chapter Three: Location, Location, Location about Paco Underhill and his retail anthropology research? Underhill found that an effective way to get shoppers attention is to create displays that have reflective surfaces (mirrors, chrome, silver, etc.). Keep in mind the direction of traffic flow around the aisles of your mall, and then create your reflective display so that shoppers will face it as they move through the aisle. If you get traffic from both directions, create two displays, one on each end of the booth.

• Place your best merchandise at eye level. Shoppers travelling the aisles of your mall glance at eye level first; if they see nothing that they're interested in at first glance then they will keep moving.

• Don't overcrowd your booth. I've seen booths that were so crowded that I didn't want to enter the space for fear of breaking something. Allow enough room for at least two people to enter your booth and browse. Most of your items should be visible from the aisle.

• Use professional signs. Antique malls are full of hand-written signs that scream "this booth is owned by an amateur who's too cheap to buy a real sign". Have your signs done at a print shop and use letters that are big enough to be read from the aisle. If you can't afford a print shop, at least print them from your computer using good quality card-stock paper. The next time you're in a department store, pay attention to their signs: what they say, where they are placed, what colors are used, and how the lettering is done. Department stores spend a lot of money on signage and they know how to display signs properly.

•   Create signs that will draw browsers into your booth. For example, if you have an object that can't be seen from the aisle you might place a sign above it that reads "What is this?" or "What do you call this?" or "Do you remember these?" Then place a big red arrow on the sign that points to the object. Natural curiosity will pull people into your booth.

•   Never use signs that read "Everything in this booth X% off". Such signs are interpreted as meaning "we need to sell something fast". Instead, offer discounts on select merchandise. Hopefully, you'll also sell something at full price and keep your profit margins up.

•   Keep your merchandise fresh (or at least looking fresh). Change your displays around weekly; move up what was down, what was on the right to the left, and so on. As you move things around, dust and clean.

• More lighting equals more visibility. Get rid of any dark spots. Sometimes, mall owners frown on having too much light because it will make their electric bill go up. If that's the case in your mall, offer to put in track lighting that uses LED bulbs. LED bulbs use less electricity and can be operated at minimal cost. Or, offer to pay higher rent to pay for the extra electricity used. Or, pay higher rent AND use LED bulbs. The point is this: keeping your booth well-lit will help you sell more.

If you'll apply the above suggestions, your booth will attract more attention than other booths in your mall. Many mall dealers cram as much merchandise into their booth as they can; then they sit back and hope that it sells. Oddly, enough of it sells to keep the mall open and the dealers in business. Imagine how much business can be done if you put a little effort into your displays!

There's one more tactic that you can use that will put you at "the head of the class" in antique mall merchandising: QR codes.

You've no doubt seen QR codes; they're everywhere. They look like this:

The idea behind QR codes is that shoppers wanting to know more about an item can snap a picture of the code with their smartphone, and the QR code will take them to a web page dedicated to the item. The web page describes the item and offers background information, a "sales pitch" if you want to give one, and a "Buy Now" discount coupon if you wish to offer one. Best of all, you can create a "Make me an offer" link to your email or text message. Once customers realize that they can connect directly to a booth's owner (instead of the just the checkout clerk) they will feel more comfortable about buying from you.

Put yourself in your customer's position: If you were "on the fence" about making a purchase, but had a question, wouldn't you appreciate an answer? How many customers (who would normally walk away) would buy if someone was there at that moment to answer questions, give a little history of the item, and build value to justify the price? How many browsers would be turned into buyers?

A QR code can provide you with the sales help that your mall management cannot. Adding QR codes to your price tags provides you with a "silent salesman" that works for you every hour that your mall booth is open. Best of all, they can be generated for free at qrstuff.com, printed onto stickers, and attached to your price tags.

Lest you think I'm going too far out on a limb with my enthusiasm for QR codes, consider that roughly two out of three[5] (72%) of the shoppers who visit your antique mall have smartphones, and they use them.

To use QR codes, you will need a web page for each item you code. Most businesses using QR codes have their own website, and the code sends the shopper to their site. But you need not go to all that trouble; you can create a landing page for each of your products on Etsy, eBay, or other online sellers. You'll spend a couple of hours learning the ropes on each of these sites, but that's less time than you would spend creating a website. To use third-party sites will require you to set up an account and take some photos. Once that's done, you'll have the added advantage of being able to sell directly on these marketplaces.

How hard is it to print QR codes, when you are doing most of the other work (photos and descriptions)

---

[5] www.statista.com/statistics/201183/forecast-of-smartphone-penetration-in-the-us/

anyway? Consumers demand product information. Antique mall dealers who deliver information in a timely fashion will find that their sales increase and their customer base grows.

Conclusion: Drive Your Business

Benjamin Franklin once said: "Drive thy business or it will drive thee".

Franklin learned that lesson while working in retail.

Benjamin is famous for his accomplishments - author, printer, politician, postmaster, scientist, inventor, and Founding Father among them. But what is not so well-known is that as a young man Franklin worked for Thomas Denham, a Philadelphia merchant who used Ben as retail clerk and bookkeeper.

Young Benjamin "earned his stripes" counting inventory, waiting on customers, and adding up profits. He learned the hard way that if a retailer doesn't take charge of his business then the business will take charge of him.

Franklin knew how to buy to right to sell right. He knew how much inventory was needed in his employer's shop. As a bookkeeper, he understood the relationship between inventory, margins, and profits. And, those lessons served him well in his own endeavors.

As you begin your own adventure as an antique mall dealer, you will notice things you hadn't previously noticed. You'll observe customers as they move through your mall, and you'll notice where they stop and what they look at. When you enter a department store, you'll notice how displays are arranged, and how signage is executed. And, you'll see antique stores where you never noticed them before. As psychologists are fond of saying, "motivation affects perception".

It won't be long before the topics covered in this book become second nature to you. You'll find yourself at an auction or a flea market and you'll compute every price and every bid in terms of your own retail markup. Over time, you'll learn to trust your hunches about what to buy and how much to charge.

Learn the principles covered in this little book until you know them by heart; they provide a solid foundation for successful retailing. For a wider range of topics on retailing antiques and collectibles, follow my business column Behind the Gavel in each edition of Antique Trader Magazine, or visit my website at sellmoreantiques.com

About the Author

Wayne Jordan is a Virginia-licensed Auctioneer, Certified Personal Property Appraiser, and Accredited Business Broker. He specializes in helping those in the antique and vintage trades sell more, manage better, and plan effectively.

Wayne has owned two retail stores, operated several Antique Mall booths, and displays regularly at Fairs and Antique Shows. He writes based on over 45 years' experience in retailing and consignment.

Since 2009, his business column Behind the Gavel has appeared bi-weekly in Antique Trader Magazine. His articles have appeared regularly in WorthPoint.com and in other trade publications.

Wayne is the author of The Business of Antiques published by Krause Books, Consignment Gold Rush: The Ultimate Startup Guide, Relocate for Less and the bestselling Antique Mall Profits for Dealers and Dabblers, both published by Learning Curve Books.

Wayne's auctioneering travels have taken him across the U.S. from Florida to Alaska, and internationally to sixteen countries from Russia to Panama. He has sold a variety of goods at auction: cars, real estate, jewelry, fine art, antiques, business assets, and estate property.

Wayne has held the professional designations of Certified Estate Specialist; Accredited Auctioneer of Real Estate; Certified Auction Specialist, Residential Real Estate and Accredited Business Broker. He has held state licenses in Real Estate and Insurance.

Wayne is an accomplished antiques restorer. His work can be found in the Museum of Virginia Military Institute, the Maryland Governor's Mansion, and fine homes and institutions throughout the Mid-Atlantic States.

What Readers are Saying

About **The Business of Antiques: How to Succeed in the Antiques World** by Wayne Jordan

My decision to give this book a five-star rating was based on the valuable information included...I would recommend this book to anyone wanting to know more about the antiques business. Knowledge is power after all.

"Husband originally found and read this book from the library, found is so informative that he requested I order it for him."

About **Antique Mall Profits for Dealers and Dabblers** by Wayne Jordan:

"Great advice for sellers, whether newbie or veteran. Easy to read. I've been a dealer for 20+ years and picked up a couple "hot tips" that were new to me. And some of the other info I needed to be reminded of, so the book definitely was worth my time to read, and I'll reread it again when my sales are in a slump. Thanks for the kick in the you-know-what, Mr. Jordan!

"An absolute "must read" before you start a business, especially an antiques booth business. Good basic info, well written, easy to understand and implement.

I just wish I could purchase a hard copy to have on hand as a good reference."

P. Roberts

"I am going to spend the recommended time analyzing my business plan - especially the inventory management ideas. Especially the concepts I read on the buying, inventory analysis and marketing described in this great little book. Thanks in advance for the insights and thought-provoking business advice. Well worth the time I spent reading it."

About Wayne's column **Behind the Gavel** in Antique Trader Magazine

"I've been reading your articles in the Antique Trader for several years now… I admire your column and appreciate your expertise! I just retired from teaching marketing at the State University of New York at Plattsburgh....and have always found your marketing advice to be brilliant! I grew up in a family where my parents had an antique and secondhand furniture store in…NY and that is where my love of antiques began. I wish you all the best and hope you will continue to write your articles for many years to come!

"Your columns are the highlight of Antique Trader. You use firsthand knowledge, industry data and logic to draw conclusions about the business of collecting rather than speculating"   J.P.

"Wayne: great article on pricing...As always, I look forward to your articles. Agree or not, they are always interesting and informative reading" R.B

More from Wayne Jordan

Find more tips from Wayne on selling antiques and vintage goods at:

Wayne's blog: http://sellmoreantiques.com

Wayne's business column **Behind the Gavel** in Antique Trader Magazine

Wayne's Feature Articles on antiques & collectibles at WorthPoint

More books from Wayne Jordan:

The Business of Antiques: How to Succeed in the Antiques World, published by Krause Books, available in both print and Kindle editions

Relocate for Less!: How to Save Money on Van Line Charges, published by Learning Curve books.

Consignment Gold Rush: The Ultimate Startup Guide available in print and Kindle editions

www.ingramcontent.com/pod-product-compliance
Lightning Source LLC
Chambersburg PA
CBHW072200170526
45158CB00004BB/1719